D1720059

Verlag für engagierte Literatur

Wir danken allen genannten und ungenannten Förderern,
die durch Patenschaften und Spenden
ermöglicht haben, dass den Kindern und Jugendlichen des
Child of Mercy Orphanage Centre (COMOC) in Likoni, Kenia,
dieses Buch zur Verfügung gestellt werden kann.
Insbesondere danken wir

der Stadt Vechta

www.vechta.de

der Volksbank Vechta

der Bürgerstiftung Vechta

**❯❯ Bürgerstiftung
Vechta**

der Firma Big Dutchman, Vechta

Big Dutchman.

und dem Verein Kultur lebt e.V., Vechta

Kultur lebt e.V.

Jump like a Kangaroo

Texte von Kindern und Jugendlichen des
Child of Mercy Orphanage Centre (COMOC)
in Likoni, Kenia

Herausgegeben von
Thalia-Anna Hampf

Jump like a Kangaroo
Texte von Kindern und Jugendlichen des
Child of Mercy Orphanage Centre (COMOC) in Likoni, Kenia
Herausgegeben von
Thalia-Anna Hampf
Geest-Verlag, Vechta-Langförden 2019

© 2019 Geest, Vechta
Verlag: Geest-Verlag, Lange Straße 41a,
49377 Vechta-Langförden

Druck: Geest-Verlag
Alle Rechte vorbehalten

ISBN 978-3-86685-703-2

Printed in Germany

Wenn unsere Ohren verlernt haben zuzuhören
Thalia-Anna Hampf

Wir hören uns unglaublich gerne über unsere Probleme reden und haben dabei verlernt, richtig zuzuhören. Dabei vergessen wir manchmal, wie gut wir es eigentlich haben und dass es an anderen Orten auf dieser Welt ganz anders aussieht.

Für drei Monate war ich in Likoni, Kenia, im Child of Mercy Orphanage und habe dort gelebt und gearbeitet. Mir war es wichtig, mit den Kindern und Jugendlichen (8 bis 19 Jahre) einige kreative Projekte zu verwirklichen, durch die sie sich selbst ausdrücken können. Neben Musik und verschiedenen Spielen ist auch dieses Buchprojekt entstanden.

An vielen Tagen haben wir uns gemeinsam hingesetzt und zu verschiedensten freien Schreibanlässen geschrieben, die ich meist vorgegeben habe. Es kam auch vor, dass die Kinder eine ganz eigene Idee entwickelt haben, zu der geschrieben wurde. Nach einer intensiven Schreibphase durfte jedes Kind freiwillig seinen Text vorlesen und wir kamen darüber ins Gespräch. Besonders mit den jüngeren Kindern habe ich viel an den Texten gearbeitet und ihnen bei Fragen auch bezüglich der Sprache geholfen. Jedoch liegt das Hauptaugenmerk bei diesem Schreibprojekt nicht auf der grammatikalischen Korrektheit, sondern darauf, seine Gefühle auszudrücken und über Themen schreiben zu können, die einen interessieren. Aus diesem Grund wurden die Texte größtenteils unberührt gelassen und nur wenig korrigiert. Dadurch, dass aus allen Texten ein Buch entsteht, sehen die Kinder und Jugendlichen, dass ihre Worte Gewicht haben, gedruckt und gelesen werden. Ich habe das Gefühl, eine Menge gegeben aber noch viel mehr gelernt und zurück bekommen zu haben. Die Kinder und Jugendlichen stecken voller Kreativität und Neugierde. Ein Junge kam jeden Tag zu mir, um zu fragen, wann wir wieder zusammen schreiben wollen. Es gibt eine Menge Potential, das manchmal nur einen kleinen Anstoß braucht, um aufzublühen.

Wenn unsere Ohren verlernt haben zuzuhören, müssen die Stimmen eben lauter werden.

When our ears have forgotten to listen
Thalia-Anna Hampf

We enjoy listening to ourselves talking about our problems but forget how to really listen. Sometimes we forget how comfortable our life is and that this is not guaranteed in other parts of the world.

For three months, I lived and worked in Likoni, Kenya, in the Child of Mercy Orphanage. It was important to me to realize some creative projects with the children and teenagers (8 to 19 year olds), through which they could express themselves. In addition to music and various games, this book project was also created.

On many days we sat down together and wrote in response to session and ideas which I mostly gave. It also happened that the children developed their very own idea, which they wrote about. After an intensive process of writing, each child was allowed to volunteer to read his or her own text and we got to talk about it. Especially with the younger children I worked a lot on the texts and helped them with questions also concerning the language. However, the main focus of this writing project is not on grammatical correctness, but on the young people expressing their feelings and writing about the topics that interest them. For this reason, most of the texts were left untouched and only slightly corrected. By making a book from all the texts, the children and teenagers see that their words are impressive, printed and read.

I think that I gave a lot but I know that I got much more back and learned a lot for myself. The children and teenagers are full of creativity and curiosity. Every day a boy came to me and asked when it's time to write together again. There is a lot of potential, that sometimes only needs a little nurturing to blossom.

When our ears have forgotten to listen, the voices have to get louder.

Table of contents

Let´s have a journey

Patrick M.

Trip with a motorboat
Kevin

I spent my holiday. I wanted to spend my holiday nicely. I was happy as a king. When I was in the bathroom I showered. I was happy because I knew I would be in the motorboat. The following day when I woke up I went to my bathroom. I washed my face. After that I had my breakefast. At seven o'clock, I packed my clothes and my shoes. I waited for the Matatu to the Ukunda Beach. When I reached the Ukunda Beach I took the motorboat. I started my journey to China. When I was in the motorboat I saw some sharks, some whales, turtles, catfish, lionfish and dragonfishs etc. I was happy to see some sharks. I saw some mammals like whales and black platipus. When I was at the motorboat I had some drinks like mango juice and banana juice. I saw an island and some snow and a white bear and tiger in the snow. I was so happy to see some animals in the snow. I took two pictures of the animals. I will never forget the journey.

Three journeys
John

In China it rains everywhere. The houses are up from the water. You know why people in China build houses from in the water? Because floods are everywhere in China
Another journey: In India there is not a lot of food. People like to plant. Most of the people like to plant maize and green grams in India.
My third journey was to Argentina. When I got there, I found people love to play football. Have you seen a footballer? Now you can see a footballer called Messi.

JB on travel
Junior

In the holiday in August I was so excited because I was going to India. When the school was closed I was in a hurry because my mother told me to hurry and pack my bag. I went to the school bus at three o'clock. When I reached my bedroom, the first thing I did was to take a long shower. Then I took my smooth towel. I wiped myself, and I wore my shorts and my shirt on which is written Justin Bieber or JB – my nickname. Then I was ready to eat my favorite meal called ugali and beans with meat. It is delicious and the best food in the world. In the middle of midnight I woke up from a loud "BANG". I was in a dream in India.

Orphanage?
Alice

It was at December and November holidays, I was in the middle of the ocean. I wanted to go to all countries. I had a superboat. I went to India. The people of India were very kind. I went to a park. The animals were nice. I saw a lion, tiger, giraffe, leopard, monkey, baboon, and other animals. At night I built a tent and then I slept. When I woke up in the morning, I showered and went to my superboat. Then I went to Spain. I met a person called Paco. He was a very nice guy. He bought chips for me and chicken. It was so delicious. Then we went to drink soda. The soda was nice. I went to his house. It was a nice house. He had 1000 children. I thought it was an orphanage. I was shocked. I fainted. In the morning I went to my superboat. Then I went to Germany. In Germany I met a person called Margi. She was a nice girl. She bought meat, potatos and Ugali for me. It was nice. I went to her house. She had 800 children. I thought that it was an orphanage. I was shocked. I fainted.

A big adventure
Harrison

It was in the evening when we were sailing. My father, my mother, my sisters and brothers and I. Suddenly we were in the middle of the ocean and we saw a little island and it was dark in the night. Suddenly we hit a very hard rock and our boat broke into two pieces. My father, mother, sisters, and brothers died but I was lucky to swim until the shore of the island. On the shore, I decided to sleep but I was wet. Because I was too tired I slept anyway. Some little men came to take some water from the ocean and they saw me on the shore. They thought I was a giant but I was as short as them because I was a child. I lived with them for three months. They found that I was a kind man to them, so they went and showed me a secret place which none of them were able to open. So I tried it and suddenly it opened and they saw something shining. It was gold and a superboat. It was only me who had the experience to drive boats, so they told me to go to the ocean and try to drive it. It was very sad for them that they saw me driving very fast and left them alone on the island. Then I went to the middle of the Pacific Ocean, and I didn't know where to go because I was in the middle of the ocean and the Pacific Ocean is the biggest ocean in the world. Then I covered myself with a hard glass and entered the water and decided to look at the animals who live in the water. I saw: lionfish, turtles, sharks, dolphins, and many other fishes and shells. While I was looking at animals in the sea, I reached the shore of the Asian continent. That is when I saw that my family is not dead. I thought they were dead but they were not and I was happy as a king. Then they helped me to get out of the superboat and carried it home. They told me their story, that there was a ship which was passing and asked to help. I was so happy when I heard their story. And they told me to tell them the story of the journey with the superboat but I was so shy that I didn't tell them.

Something I learned
Neema

One day when we were still on the journey I saw many people with different colours and many things like different countries and animals. My journey was from Kenya to Germany. I saw many things and learned many things from them. The languague is different from ours. In Kenya we speak Kiswahili and English but in Germany it's different from here.

A journey to Spain
Dorcus

My name is Dorcus. This is all about a journey to Spain. Once I was on the sea. Then at last I found myself in a city called Malaga. Once I got there, I thought the people there were friendly, lovely, and caring. One family looked after me and they decided to help me. I saw that this family was caring so they explained to me that they shall do anything that I will ask them to do. The saying "all is well that ends well" isn't wrong. The family taught me how to cook "tarta de patata". Then they told me that they will find a football team for me so I can develop my talent. They took me to Valencia but they found no team in Valencia so they decided to take me to Madrid. I decided to join the team and my first game was in Barcelona. There we played with the girls from Barca. It was enjoyable playing with people whom I have never met in my life. A house was given to me in which I slept three nights. After we had finished the game we went back home. We practiced. As you know practice makes perfect. I went back to Malaga. We were invited to a party in Tivoli World. At Tivoli World we saw a lot of musicians like Daddy Yankee, Luis Fonsi, Justin Bieber, Cardi B and many more. I had never imagined that. I know that when you travel you know more things than being idle.

All this were just dreams and wishes that I shall see Spain. I shall see a lot of countries in the world. Doing this is not impossible. It only needs working hard and harder and you shall do this in your future. Toil is just a simple thing. Everybody can be a hero or a heroine. Focusing in your life is what matters and also praying. That moment you will shine bright like a diamond in the sky and keep knowing that the sky is not the limit.

Me, Myself and I

Patrick C.

My life
Blanice

Hello, my name is Natasha Blanice and I am 17 years old. I stay in Child of Mercy Children's Home with my four siblings. Next year I will be in form 3. After next year I will go to sit my final exams which will be in November 2020. I hope to see that day. I will be able to go to a university and I hope I will. This is one of my dreams – to go to a university. I hope one day I will be a bank accountant or a lawyer. I would like to help orphans and widows in the future. Also I would like to visit Brazil, Jamaica and many other countries in the world. Hope that the almighty God help me through my dreams. My hobbies are reading books, riding bike and swimming. I like swimming because we are near the beach. My talents are playing football only.

A day at the beach
John

My friend is called Thalia. She is a good friend like you have not seen yet. When she came here she was a good volunteer. The first day in COMOC she told us: "Let's go to the beach". When we were on the way we talked and talked and we were very happy when we reached the beach. We swim in the sea. We swim and swim. Everybody enjoy the beach and we were all happy!

My plans
Jane

Hello, I'm Jane. My nickname is Lopez. I am 13 years old. I like dancing and singing. My hobby is playing football. I like eating so much. When I grow up I would like to be a dancer or a musician. But when I finish my studies I would like to be a teacher. Being a teacher is a good job. I would like to visit many countries like America, Australia, France, Germany, Tanzania etc. I would like to live with my peers or my sisters. I have lots of friends. E.g. Salma, Naomi, Terry, Khadija, Camila (Tabby), Alshakeys (Aisha), Stephen, Ammy, Musa, Razack and many more.

When I grow up
Aisha

My name is Aisha and I like calling myself Alshakeys because Alshakeys is near Aisha. When I grow up I want to be a nurse or a person which travels all over the world. I like myself because I always do good things for myself. I like playing with my brothers and sisters because I love them. I live in a centre. I like the director and the other staff. They usually provide something big for me. I love the centre and I know one day when God answers my prayers and I have my own money I will not forget the orphanage. That is my dream. I want my dream to become true.

My team
Brian

My hobby is football. I like playing football because in this world with football you can go far. Some people like Christiano Ronaldo have become rich because of playing football. I have also a football team known as Ocean Stars.

Dear friend
Brenda

My friend is called Salim Sudi. He is in class four west. He is fourteen years old. He is my best friend. This letter is to my best friend. My name is Brenda Nangi. He likes playing football with me. His favorite school is Mrima Primary School. He loves me and also I love him very much. I also have other friends called Amina Amar, Lucy, Sofia, Nyamawi in Mrima Primary School. I love them so much. Bye.

Share a hobby
Tabby

My name is Tabby aka Camila M. I like and adore this name because of the series known as Riverdale. I really like the way she acts. My hobby is playing football. Since I was young I like it and I would practise so hard to know how to dribble. I took this hobby from my mom cause my mom also likes playing football. I also like watching soaps, opera movies or love stories.

My home
Zulfa

My name is Zulfa, I am twelve years old. I live in Child of Mercy. It is a nice place. I like this place as my home. In Comoc there are 40 children. They are like my brothers and sisters. In Child of Mercy we have a big house. We have rooms of boys, girls and aunties. And we also have volunteers. We have a manager, Mama, aunties and uncles who take care of us. I like them as my parents.

Future Life
Sarah

Hi, my name is Sarah Jonathan and I am 17 years old. I stay in Child of Mercy Children's Home. Next year in 2019 I will finish up with my high school studies and I will be aiming to go to Mount Kenya University in Thika, Kenya. There I will grow to be one of the professional nurses or journalists. I would like to help all the helpless people in the world. I would like to make a change that will stick on people's hearts and make people love each other and stay as one family. My dream countries are Germany, Australia and Mexico. I really admire to go to these countries. I hope that I will work for one of these countries one day. May the almighty God help me to fulfil my dreams through my hard work and become one of the most respected ladies in the world. Thank you.

About me
Sengale

Hi, my name is Sengale. I am eight years old. I'm in class two and next year I will be going into class three. My talent is to be a basketballer. My favorite food is chapati and samosa.

Football
Aisha

My name is Alshakey. I like playing football and my friends always join me. I like football because football is famous. That's why I like it. My friends always go to football practise and I always join. I like watching Kwese (TV-channel) because there are sports on Kwese and I always see the way how they play. I like to see famous people like Messi, Neymar, Özil, Ronaldo and Isco. They are the best footballers.

Winner and money
John

My dream is to be a football player. You know why I want to be a football player? Because football is life and football makes money. Player get more money than the president. A famous player gets
10.000.000 and a president gets 10.000. But do you know a name of any player? Messi, Christiano, Neymar. Do you know any French player? France won the world cup in Russia. The cup which France won was for God. My favorite team is Chelsea. I like Chelsea because they become the winner.

To Sarah
Sharon

Dear friend,
my name is Sharon. I am so glad writing this letter to my best friend known as Sarah. She is 17 years old and we both live in an orphanage – Child of Mercy Orphanage Centre. She is very cute and helpful to me. She shows love to me and sometimes she encourages me when I am sad. Sometimes we share food and even walk together as friends. We both met in an orphanage when she was four years old and I was six years old but now I am 18 years old and she is 17 years old. We both will do our Kenya Certificate of secondary education. That will be the last class of high school and then we will go to a university. But I am glad that we are getting educated from the orphanage and I have got other friends from school and they are Claris and Linet.

Netball
Zulfa

My best hobby is playing netball. I like playing netball very much. In our school we play netball. Netball is a game which is played in in two teams. That game is very funny but we are always playing a friendly game. Some of the people play by beating others. In Kenya they play an unfriendly game when they don't know each other. My hobby is very nice. I like it very much. I love playing netball very much. It is my best hobby.

Music, travel and books
Sarah

Hello, my name is Sarah Jonathan. I like traveling and listening to music. I also enjoy myself while reading storybooks. By traveling I will be able to see things that I have never seen before and maybe learn about them and grow up by already knowing them. By listening to music I take myself away from many things and when I'm angry I can calm down while listening to music and forget my anger. By reading storybooks I teach myself how to be busy always and I also teach myself new vocabularies and words. While reading some storybooks I learn what life is and end up working hard for my life to be better.

My hobbies
Tabby

Hello from far away! My name is Tabby aka Camila M. I am 15 years old. My hobby is watching soaps with love stories and my talent is playing football. In my future I would like to be an air hostess so I can travel from one country to another. My dream countries are just three. They are Italy, Germany and Spain. I like Germany cause my relatives live in Germany and Italy. I hope that my dreams would be fulfilled by God one day. I also like watching indian movies. My favorite actors are Kajol and Shah Rukh Khan. I really like this two Indians because when they act they express their feelings to each other. I really love Kajol. I hope one day I can meet her!

Dreams and Nightmonsters

Junior

The nightmare
Abdul

Two years ago there was a boy who had a bad nightmare. He has a big doll. This doll liked monsters. If he sleeps at night he has a very bad dream. One day the boy was in the hospital, sleeping in his bed, when the dream came again. The dream talked: "Who are you?" and the boy said: "My name is Alex and I am in the hospital". Then the monster came out of the door and caught the head of the boy. The boy woke up very fast, scared by the nightmare and the doll. So the boy cut his doll and slept again. Now the nightmare is not coming again. So this is the end of the story about nightmonsters and night-mares.

We should not have a monster doll or CDs of monsters. Can you listen to me please! I am telling you the truth of night monsters. I can draw for you a night monster.

It has:
- One red eye
- Two Horns
- Sharp teeth
- Two legs
- Two hands

Fairytail
Kay

One day, on a Sunday morning, the sun was shining like a bright star. Then I went to take the best shower in the Frog's Kingdom. After a few minutes I went and put on my uniform and started walking to school. Then I went to pick up my best friend on my way to school. Then he said this: "Do you know that we are going to close school tomorrow?" It was evening. In the night when the children were all asleep a light entered the room. When it came to rest, you could see it was a fairy. Then you heard someone calling Tinker Bell. A moment later Peter dropped in. "Where is my shadow?", he said. "Over there", said Tinker Bell. When Peter caught up with it, he thought that he and his shadow would join together like two drops of water. When they didn't, he shuddered and sat on the floor and cried. Wendy asked Peter where he lived. "Second on the right, and then straight on till morning.", he said. "What a funny address!", Wendy said. "No it isn't!", said Peter. "I mean is it that what they put on the letters?", Wendy said. Then it was morning. I went and told my friends everything what happened. I told them that it was just a dream.

Nightlife
Lewis

I sleep at night, I play at night. I do my work at night and I read at night. I eat at night, I see dreams at night. I eat fish at night.

In my house
Patrick C.

Yesterday I saw the monster in the toilet. Another day I opened and closed my eyes and went into the house. "Go away I don't want you in my house please!".

Monsters
John

One day I was asleep and dreamed about night monsters I saw in my dream. The second day my father saw the monster trying to kill my mother but the dream was true. So I tried to fight with the monster. When you pray, God believes you. Pray when you are in bed, and when you are dreaming you can talk in your sleep and even make signs. And many times you talk about bad movies like vampire movies you have watched. Have you seen monsters? Please don't watch movies which are evil. Please I am beging you world. Please, please I am begging you. Don't try to see movies when you are going to sleep.

Three days later a boy decided to sleep in an old house. He was scared that he would dream bad dreams. He decided when he is sleeping, he would put on the light and pray. The boy was called John. He was born in 2008 and is still alive. Now he is ten years old. Now he is in the country which is called wonderland. He is enjoying his life. He has a family and have seen a ghost – one side is red the other side is green. His face was from an evil man and it's still moving.

Monster house
Junior

My name is Junior Baraka. One night, I had a dream that I was in a monster house. It was dark and it had spiderwebs and big rats. When you said something the sound echoed. When I went to the kitchen I saw a head of a human being and his legs. After that I was very scared. When it was lunch time the monster came to the kitchen.

Never forget
Aisha

It was dark in the evening. I went to take a bath. When I reached the bathroom, I entered inside and turned on the shower. The water in the shower was cool and fresh. When I finished showering I took my towel and went inside the room. I felt fresh like a cucumber. I wore my sleeping clothes – the pyjama. I was lying in my bed, waiting to fall asleep. When I was asleep, I dreamed that there is a man who likes raping children. One day the man found me alone outside on my way to buy something. The man took me and raped me. I started screaming and there was no one to help me. Everybody was asleep. That is what I dreamed. I will never forget that day. I will never forget that dream.

John

Let it snow

Junior

Facts
Derrick

A bear lives in snow in Africa. There is snow on Mount Kenya.
There is yellow snow which should not be eaten.

Cold countries
Blanice

I like snow but I know it is very cold. In the future I would like to visit a country which is cold. It will be Canada because I heard there it is very cold. In Canada I will visit a hotel called Ice Hotel. I heard everything is ice! Hope to go there.

Love you
Zulfa

Snow, snow, snow, Ohoo you are cold, I love you
you make us happy by playing with you, ohoo snow, I love
you
There is nothing like you snow love you
nothing that I don't love about snow, ohoo Snow you are
good
I will love you

Hot and cold
John

One day I was in Mombasa. There was no snow in Mombasa. You can find much snow up on the hill. Kilimanjaro has a lot of snow. Even on Mount Everest is a lot of snow. I go to China everywhere around the city. I climbed up the roof of an house and even up the hill. My country is Kenya. It's warm. My city is Mombasa. It is so hot. People are hot but sometimes it is cold in August when we have holidays. When we go to school and the pupils are learning, they feel cold. When they go to school, they wear heavy clothes. When they are talking, they remove something. When you wake up you go to shower. Then you feel cold and even the water is cold – you shake. It means it is very cold. I love my story about snow. I love snow.

Snow games
Harrison

In snow you can play so many games, like making houses, making a palace, throwing snowballs to others, fishing, and many other games. I know Africa has no snow but there is snow on top of the mountains like Mount Kenya, Mount Killimanjaro, Mount Rwenzori and many other mountains. People are playing with snow. One day I went to Europe. I decided to visit Mount Everest because it is the largest mountain in the world and has so much snow.

We climbed the mountain with Thalia. We climbed up to the top of Mount Everest. We climbed for one month and nineteen days. It was so interesting!

Snow day
Abdul

Our country has no snow so one day I go to Germany. I find much snow there now. I am ready to go to my house because it's snow day. Now I must wear a lot of clothes. My story is about snow.

Winter
Junior

My name is Junior. My favorite season is snow (winter). I like snow very much because you make a snowman and you can play snowball with others because snow is like mud. You can go into the ice but it is dangerous to swim in iced water. You can be covered with ice all over your body.

Junior

Snow places
Brian

When you walk on the mountains in the cold countries like Germany and Italy, you will find some snow. Most people in the places where you can find snow, like to play with the snow. Also some people always model things using the snow. I have never seen any snow but I have read books and watched movies about snow.

When snow melts it changes into water. In our country there is one place known as Mount Kenya. That is the only place where you can find snow. At our home I use to watch movies about snow. There are some animals which are living in the snow. One of the animals is a bear and the bear is my favorite animal even if I have never seen him before!

Snowy
Jane

Snow is very rare in Africa, but in Australia, Germany, and many other countries it's very snowy. We Africans like it because we don't have it. Europeans like it too, because they have it.

I like snow because you can play a lot of games. You can make a snow man, play balls with it. If you like it, crown it.

You can not eat snow cause it's very cold. You can play in the snow but not much because it's cold. Do you like snow as I do?

Snow dates
Zulfa

In our country Kenya we don't have snow. I wish we had snow in our country – but no. Snow is found in some countries. Some snow is on the mountain but I have never seen snow. One day my dream will come true and I will go to some countries to see snow. Snow is very cold but I like snow. You can find snow in many countries but not in Kenya. Kenya doesn't have snow. It is very funny. In Germany they have snow in winter from December to February and sometimes in March. It is the only country from which I know the snow dates. I know some people who don't like snow and some who like. In Kenya are some mountains which have snow like Mount Kenya but I have never seen them. If snow could be in Kenya I could like snow very much. In snow time people wear sweaters, gloves, trousers, socks and skates. My name is Zulfa, I am twelve years old and live in Child of Mercy. I like that. In some years I would like to travel to some countries where you can find snow. I hope my dream will come true.
Thank you!

Little Snow
Ali

I like snow. Snow is not in Kenya. It is only on mountains. I only know that about snow. I like snow.

Junior

To my parents

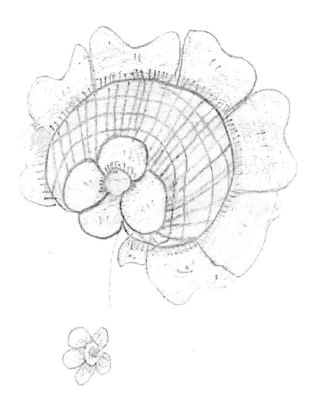

Neema

My plan
Christine

Dear Dad,
Hello! I hope that you are doing good there in Jamaica and everything is going well. I really miss you very much. I hope we can be together here in Kenya. Dad, even if you are there, please remember to send us something because here in Kenya is not much rain now and the food is hard to get. The price is high. Please dad I need some help from you, because I have a plan and that plan is about helping the kids in need and also the poor. I want to build an orphanage for the kids because some children of Kenya are not going to school, and some have no place to live. Even no clothes to wear. So please Dad can you speak to your friends about that issue so that we can find a way to help the children?

Dad can you have a heart for helping the ones in need? When you help, God will bless you and he will also open all the ways for you. He will also bless your work and also us, your children will get the blessing. Dad I have a heart for helping. Dad remember that I really love you. Don't worry about us we are ok and we are doing good and we are happy as a king. I hope that you will receive the letter with a lot of smile. Have a nice time.

Your lovely girl Tina B.

Dear Dad
Alice

Hii Dad. How are you there in America? We miss you Dad. We hope you are fine Dad. We also hope that you will come to take us. Mum always cooks nice food for us there in America. Daddy what are you doing now? Aunty Rebecah is living with uncle Paco in London.
From: your lovely daughter & son Alice & Ronaldo
To: Daddy

My visit
Harrison

Dear Dad and Mom,
How are you there in Germany? I hope you are doing well in Germany. I don't think that you are sick anymore because I left you riding a wheelchair in A.L.K hospital in Germany. When I come back to Germany I want you to prepare a party for me, your son Harrison who is coming soon in December 1, 2018. Never forget that I am somwhere where I learn well, eat well, drink well and many other activities. I will be very happy when I come to Germany. Write a book or a letter for me.
From your faithful son Harrison Inziano

Without you
Tabby

I really love both my parents – my Dad and my Mom – very much. Sometimes I feel so lonely being without you. I feel like I am in my own world and planet. When I see my fellow people being happy with their families, I feel something itching in my heart, and I feel to shout so people can hear me and heal my feelings about you. I also like you and I am waiting to see my little brothers. I hope when you come to Likoni you come with my little brothers. I really want you to be here with me and keep me company. Even if you are not here with me I want you to know that I have new friends at school, and they are like a family to me. My friends are Maggy, Riziki, Hellen, Sharon and Venessa. I wish I could search for you wherever you are and also explain my problems to you. Mom and Dad I need your hugs and kisses. I know you are working so hard to satisfy my little brothers but I hope one day I could see your lovely faces.

Greetings
Zulfa

Dear Dad,
I hope you are fine. I really miss you very much. It is very nice here. I wish I was with you but because of work I am not there. Goodbye I love you From: Zulfa Bakari To: Dad

Hey parents!
(anonym)

I feel awful when you argue about family issues. It normally irritates me sometimes. I wish that I could be the problem solver, but on the other hand I see that it's very hard to be involved in parent issues. I can not involve myself with something which is not mine. But I love you all. I don't want to stand between you two. Love is an important thing in the world. So you come together and solve these problems. Think of us too. Your problems involve us too. It's hard. Put us out of them by not arguing.

Come back
Christine

Mother what have I done to you Your lovely child – you have
left me And ran away – you have left me With the sadness
Now I dont have a mother Who can take good care of me
Please mum come back to me

Mum I still need your love and you smile You have left only
me and dad in the house I am the one who is doing all the
things The time dad is going to look for food
I´m staying at home to do the house work Please mum come
back to me I need your love

If I went to the neighbours to play They all ran away – I really
feel pitty
If they want to eat they chase me away
In that time I really feel lonely and I'm always crying
I wish my mum could be there so I could play with her Please
mum come back to me I need your love

Mum you have carried me in your womb You brought me to
the world
Now you are running away from me
Would have been better if you haven´t brought me to the
world I need you and I love you
Please mum come back to me I need your love

Hopes
Neema

Dear Daddy,
Hello! I hope you are fine? I'm doing well here in Kenya. I eat
Ugali every day. I'm growing bigger and bigger. I hope you
will come to visit me in Kenya.
Your lovely daughter
Neema

Expression of love
Jane

To my parents – especially Mum
For all the time that I have forgotten to thank you. For all the
tears that rolled down my chubby cheeks. You swiped them
away with bitterness. For all the months you have carried me
in the womb. I have never told you that I love you. And it is
time for me to tell you the truth and hold your hands and care
for you Mum. Thank you Mum. I love you Mum.

Changing into an animal

Junior

Lonely
Zulfa

One morning I woke up early in the morning. I went to the
mirror. Then I washed my face. When I looked at the mirror
my body was changing into an animal. I started screaming. I
felt very bad to change into an animal. It was a lion. I did not
go to school. I was feeling very bad. People were scared of me
because I was a lion. I was going crazy. People ran away when
they see me. So I decided not to go to school. I hated to be an
animal because it is very dangerous. I was roaming around
the campus. I was eating bits of food which people have not
finished and threw away then. I was lonely. I was bored. But
the end of the day I went to the mirror and I was changing
back to human being. I was very happy. I started behaving
like a human being. Some people told me that I was a lion. I
said: "No, I was not an animal!" people laughed at me and I
was very disappointed. I started to cry. I started to fear. I went
to sleep. I was very very tired.

Going to the doctor
Abdul

Once upon a time I was at home and it was night. I sleep up to morning. I go to the toilet and I look in the mirror. I saw a monster face and I was very scared of my face. So I ran very fast. I ran to my mother. My mother said: "My son you're a monster! Let's go to the doctor." The ambulance came very fast and took me to hospital. The doctor said: "Your son is not sick. But he has many problems. Go and put all the mirrors out of your house because if the boy sees himself in the mirror he will change to a monster. If he changes to a monster you must catch him in a net. Take this net and go home. If he changes call us on 072983007846983 - that is the number of our phone."

A Shock
Alice

One morning I woke up in the morning. I went to the wash-room. I looked at myself in the mirror. I was changing into a fish. I started screaming and crying. My mum came and she was shocked. My mother ran and called my father. My father shouted loudly. My mum and dad started crying.

Surprise
Derrick

One day early in the morning I woke up. I went to the mirror.
I saw my face was looking like a spider. I was shocked but it
was in my dream.

At the zoo
John

One day I was walking and thinking about changing into an animal. I changed into a tiger. I went to the zoo and then the zoo man said: "This is a tiger." The first day in the park the zoo man makes the zoo ready for the people to see the tiger. I became the most famous animal in the world and my family became famous. I get a lot of money 1.000000 ksh and won 10.00000 ksh on the lotto.

John

On four legs
Blanice

One day I woke up very early in the morning and I was unable to stand on my two feet. I used both my hands and legs to go to the mirror. I could not believe what I saw with my two eyes. I saw myself as a big cat standing on the mirror. I started shouting wondering why I was a cat. My mother came and got scared and went back and fainted. My father came in and called the doctor and the doctor was afraid to catch me. I saw that I ran away near to the bush that was near our home and never wanted to see my home again.

In the night
Lewis

I wake up at night. I look at the mirror. I see a lion. I shout loudly and it was a dream. I was going to my friend at the night. I was going to the toilet. I go to see my face. It was changing into an animal face of the lion.

Scared
Patrick C.

One day I was scared of changing my face. I wake up and go
to play with other friends. At night I go to sleep. I sleep and
see myself in the mirror and went: "Rararara" and also cry and
remove me out of the house. I was scared and I was running
faster and I don't come back.

Jump up and down
Abdul

My favorite animal is a kangaroo because it jumps up and down and it has a pocket to keep his baby in the pocket. I go home, sleep on the bed and was very happy because I saw a kangaroo when I dreamed. In the morning I started to jump up and down and I don't know why. I jumped up and down and I went to the mirror. I looked at my face. I saw my face looks like a kangaroo. I was happy because I was a kangaroo now. I jumped one step and I returned to be a boy.

Wild animals
Ochieng

One day I was hungry. I like to eat. I wish I can be a pilot.
My name is giraffe. I have a long neck. My friend is tiger.
I like to play wild animals.
I like to play with a dog.
I wake up. I saw satan.
I like to play wild animals.
Like baby of simba.

Ochieng

Different
Patrick M.

One day I was going to sleep at night. I was going to the toilet. I go and see my face. It was changing into an animal. The animal who I was changing to was like a wolf. I went to the other mirror. I see that my face is still like that. I go outside. I see the people with some bicycle. They looked at me then they ran away and I asked: "Why are you afraid of me?" They tell me that I am like an animal. I feel so sad. Then I go to the other neighbour. They ran away. Then I go and sleep. My mother shouted: "There is an animal in the bed". It was a dream. I feel happy.

Beautiful
Tabby

It was early in the morning when I was washing my face after a deep sleep. When I looked at myself in the mirror I saw myself turning into a peacock. I felt really good because peacocks are the most beautiful birds I have ever seen on this planet Earth. I wish that I could show to everybody that my face and my body has turned into a peacock. I felt very proud of my face. I felt like shouting so that people can hear me.

Two stories
Junior

Version 1

It was a shiny morning when I woke up. The sun was shining like the stars up there that I saw last night. I heard the birds singing like a choir. When I was taking a shower I liked it. I looked at the mirror to brush my teeth. Then I saw my face – I was shocked. My head has changed into a giraffe's head. Then after five seconds my neck is growing so tall that I was scared. When I heard my father calling me: "You are stupid! Wake up lazy boy!" So I wake up quickly and touch my head and neck. I was very happy that I have not changed into a wild animal. After that day I like visiting the wild animals.

Version 2

It was a shiny morning. I heard the birds singing like a choir. I heard my father in the kitchen. I go and take a shower and wash my face. The water was so hot like I am going to the sun. Then I brush my teeth with my mashine brush. Looking into the mirror I was shocked that my face was looking like a giraffe's head. Then I start touching the mirror. It was a picture that my sister has put on the mirror. My sister is in the next toilet room. She is showering.

Merry Christmas
and a Happy New Year

CHRISTMASTREE

PRESENT

I LOVE CHRISTMAS

Jane

What I like
Ochieng

My name is Ochieng. When I celebrate the birthday of Jesus I like to eat Pilau. I like to celebrate holiday of Jesus. I love Jesus.

Traditions
Tabby

We always celebrate our Christmas on 25th of December. I usually prefer Christmas to be on Friday not on Sunday. On Christmas day we usually go to church, beach or town. On the day of Christmas people wear new clothes not old ones cause on Christmas day you must be well dressed. We always enjoy our Christmas.

X-Mas day
Dorcus

Christmas is a celebration which is always celebrated by most of the people in the world. It is mostly celebrated by Christians and some of the Muslims. It is celebrated because of a person called Jesus Christ. It is said that this man is born on December 25th. So people marked this as X-Mas day. It is always followed by boxing day (26th). This day was meant for opening the gifts you were given on X- Mas day. On this X-Mas day people sing songs of joy. These songs are called carols. People invite friends and relatives on this day. Most of the people just celebrate it without knowing the meaning of it. It is always happy when X-Mas comes. For X-Mas I wish to have friends who are real friends.

Christmas child
John

Christmas is a day on which people celebrate. You know why people celebrate? Because it is the birth of Jesus. We celebrate the birth of Jesus in December. When people celebrate the birth of Jesus they eat and drink a lot food and drinks. On December people go to some places like the zoo. Merry Christmas!

Reasons to celebrate
Sharon

Hi, I am Sharon from Child of Mercy Orphanage Centre. I am joining form four in 2019 and my hobby is playing football and sometimes dancing in Kenya. We normally celebrate Christmas so that we can remember how Jesus was crucified on the cross for our sins. That's why we celebrate Christmas and a Happy New Year is the symbol that God has enabled us to see another year of blessing and we also go to church for celebration.

Lesson
Alice

My name is Alice. I would like to teach you about Christmas. At Christmas people dance, drink, eat, play and give. In Kenya some people go to church. People go everywhere they want to represent themselves. People go to many places like Haller Park, Mount Kenya and other places.

Soon
Derrick

In 34 days it's Christmas. We will celebrate with a big party. I
will be happy.

In December
Brenda

My name is Branda Nyangi. I am in class four next year. I am 11 years old. In December I will be 12 years old. I want to tell you something about my happy birthday. My happy birthday is on December 25th. In December we play together. Other people visit their parents. Also in December visitors come to visit us and we welcome them. Also in December we visit places like World Waters. It is a smart place. I like that place but most of the time we visit a place called Nashville. Also this is a nice and smart place. We also eat chicken and chapati. But me I like chapati more than everything. That's my favorite food in Child of Mercy.

Celebration
Brian

New Year's Day is a happy day. Everyone celebrates all over the world because a new year has started. Some people from some other countries throw fire work during the day of Happy New Year. Happy New Year is celebrated on the first day of the year.

What we do on Christmas
Aisha

We always celebrate our Christmas holiday on 25th of December. When it is Christmas we always receive visitors and we feel happy to get visitors! When it is Christmas we always dress well and tidy and smart. When it is Christmas we celebrate the birth of Jesus who saved us and he will be the savior. I like the day of Christmas because we always eat and feel happy.
I wish you a merry Christmas!

Different places
Junior

Many people go to hot countries for their Christmas. They like swimming in the seas, they love the sunny weather. Other people go to the cold countries. They like the snow. The ice hotel in Canada is a great place for these people. Would you like a holiday in the ice hotel? Everything is ice. There are beautiful lamps. There is an ice restaurant. There are 80 flavors of ice-cream.

Prepare

Jane

On 24th December in Kenya people prepare what to eat. We decorate our houses. We put on music during the night. People don't sleep until morning. On 25th December we celebrate Jesus Christ's day. We eat and drink lots and lots of things. Some Christians go to the church to pray so that they can be forgiven their sins. But a lot of people don't pray. I am among those who pray.

Visitors
Tabby

I prefer New Year's Day more than Christmas cause on Happy New Year we are allowed to go out and walk anywhere but on Christmas we celebrate with visitors cause on December we have a lot of visitors. We play, dance, sing and eat. Happy new year!

What we like to do
Sarah

We always celebrate our Christmas on 25th of December where we really have a lot of fun. On Christmas day we always celebrate the birth of Jesus. On Christmas day we may receive visitors and have fun together with them. We may also go for a trip or to the beach to have fun. On every 1st January we also celebrate our Happy New Year and we may stay awake up to the morning and go to the beach at night to light the fireworks with other people and celebrate with them when we go to the next year. It is always fun.

What I need
William

I live in COMOC. I need clothes to wear for Christmas. We have good food. I hope Thalia, you will greet your friends in Germany. We need clothes for Christmas. I miss you Thalia. Greet your friends and also sister and brothers. And I say thank you for the instruments. I am 13 years old.

Out of the box

Kenyans food.

ugali

Cook for your friends them in Germany.

Chapati

beans

rice

mixture of Beans/maize

Juice

Sukuma

Mchicha.

Don't forget this foods.

Zulfa

Emotional music
Gladys

Music is something enjoyable in this world. The world is full of music. Totally full of different types of it. Some they build strength and give hope for the hopeless, some empower people spiritually and some also break people's emotions and remind people like leaders in the society what to do. Some nations and cities bring people together by showing them how important it is to be together. Music can be listened to at any time. When you are broken, when you are happy with your friends. Some is played on party days. Don't forget that some discourage people in life like the poor when the rich boast to themselves with what they have. This breaks poor people's hearts by thinking that they can't do it. You sing your songs and hope to encourage not to discourage. Remember we are all human.

Vegetation
Brian

Vegetation is some important thing in our life. A place without vegetation is known as desert. Without vegetation you can't get water that you could use to wash things and cook food. In Africa there is a country known as Somalia. People are dying because there is no vegetation. Without vegetation we cannot get any food and animals and we will all die. We have to plant trees in our land.

Johns Song
John

How to sing:

Education is the key people learn too much

Education is the key people learn and understand (×2)

Lion is the king of all animals and Lion is the king of the jungle (×2)

Animal meeting
Derrick

Once upon a time there lived a tiger and a monkey loving each other. The tiger liked to eat animals like bear, bison and zebra. But one day Thalia comes to see what the tiger was doing. The tiger was eating a zebra. The lion was so angry that they started fighting.

A letter
Ali

Dear Thalia,
I hope you are fine. My name is Ali and I want to tell you that you are good. I say you are good because you always take us to the beach, teach us how to write stories. I want to tell you to continue with your wonderful heart. Bye!
From your wonderful friend: Ali

The Monster Truck
Abdul

Once upon a time there was a big Monster Truck. An animal with six legs came and entered the truck so I start driving the truck. A boy was in the garage. I see the car is moving around and then there is no one in the car. So I look down and I saw the monster.
That is the end of my story.

Hungry
Sengale

U.S.A
My friend likes to eat too much food and she became fat.
Then she is starting to become thin. And then she doesn't like
to eat too much food.

Abduls Song
Abdul

I was sleeping in my bed when I saw someone catching me. I jump up and down like a kangaroo. KANGAROO!
My mother told me not to jump like kangaroo KANGAROO!
I told my mother I don't jump like kangaroo KANGAROO!
It was my dream my mother was happy. She took me to the zoo. I saw a kangaroo jump up and down and then I jump up and down. My mother saw me jumping up and down. She told me not to copy what kangaroos do. I told my mother it's very funny to copy what animals do. My mother is happy about what I am doing.
I was jumping up and down like kangaroo KANGAROO!

Skins

Tabby

My thoughts
Clement

In this life nothing is good like being good and saving the nation. But there is something on my mind whenever I sleep. In this world there is nothing worse than someone abusing you on your skin colour. We blacks have a lot of disadvantages. This includes:

I)   Discouragement of our looking
II)   Our beauty of face may not surprise others
III)   The way we look outside and inwards
IV)   Our names may also sound ugly
V)   Appearance of our states where we live

In my deep thoughts I think white people have been discouraging us blacks. They may sometimes think that we can not invent anything in this world. They just see us like non-caring human beings. Not all whites say that, but some of them take us for the less thinking man. In this life you can't only succeed through your parents wealth, but only god knows your ability. It isn't that whites are special. Some of them get married with blacks and it's gorgeous as usual. With a lot of hope we blacks want to be equal to the whites.

Welcome everyone
Sharon

Hi! I am Sharon but I like calling myself Messi because I like playing football a lot. The only thing I would like to encourage people about is that we should not be discouraged by our skin colour, because I like both colours even if it is a white skinned person. We should encourage each other regardless of skin colour because the only difference is that Africans are black skinned while the Europeans are white skinned. But we all pray to one God and God listens to everyone. We are also all equal because we all have red blood and everything that is found in a european body is also found in an african body.

I normally feel so bad when I hear that Donald Trump does not want Africans in the United States. When people from different countries come to Kenya they are normally welcomed without using discrimminations. So me I don't like racial discrimmination. When I grow up, I would like to be a rugby player and join some football teams in Kenya, and get support from European nations so I can play football for them.

Equality
Harrison

Everthing in Africa is black. People say that black is beauty, but before the world was digital, Europeans like the British and others treated us like slaves by saying that we are gorillas of Africa. In the world there is no one who is better than the other. People like the British and many other Europeans treated us like gorillas, chimpanzees, monkeys etc.

This means that they treated us like we are not humans like them. But why did they colonise us Kenyans if we are monkeys? And never forget the people who are white like the Europeans in Kenya which speak Swahili. They are called "nguchiru*". In Kenya we call every other white man from Europe, Asia, Australia etc. "Mzungu". There are some presidents which are black, like those in the union of Africa.

But the main point of this story is: no one is better than the other, it doesn't matter which colour you have. Like black.

*

Our colors
Alice

My friend is called Amina. She is a girl. Her skin colour is light brown and my skin colour is black. In our orphanage we are 40 people. We are all black, no one is white except the Mzungus. Our skin colours are different. To God we are the same.

Sugar
John

„Hi, my name is Omari."
He is in the same school as me. His skin is white. Maybe he
has eaten a lot of sugar. It is not good for people. Some people think sugar is good to eat. Maybe he likes sugar, and
that's why he eats a lot of sugar. Even some people die.
Maybe they ate bad things.

Take care
Tabby

On this planet earth there are things which are reality and not reality. We have two different colours
– black and white. I prefer both because black is normal and white people's skin is so reactive and sensible. For example they are not used to the heat and climate in Kenya. In this world most white people are known as Albino. I usually feel pity for them because they are not used to the heat. To protect themselves by putting a cap on their head. We must always love them and take care of them and remember that we are all human beings and we were created for a reason in this world. We should stop dreading and stigmatizing Albinos.
We were born on this world to shine. You should always think about others not yourself. Nothing is worse than being bad to other people. In my opinion we should live in peace in this world and know how people feel when you stigmatize then.

Black
Christine

I am black, you're black, everthing is black. Don't feel so bad about being black. Black is the colour of everthing and it's the song we always sing. Let me tell you my good friend, don't be like a person which is in the glass be like the person who is in the unity to support your colour and don't feel so bad about your colour even if you are an Albino or a European. I love my colour and my country because it represents our country and unity, so don't feel so bad about being black. Black is the colour of everthing and it's the song we always sing. Do not dread the colour of your friend, treat the person like your own sister.

Watch out
Anne

In this world are some people who have skin problems. Some of them are white in colour and some of them are black in colour. The people who are white in colour are called Albinos. They are usually in white colour. There are a lot of Albinos in Kenya but the Kenyan people are black. And the Kenyan people think that they are Europeans. In Kenya we usually call them "nguchiru". Some people may be born with black skin and when they grow up they will colour into white. Some of them can be born with white skin and if they grow up they will be very black. We should love them, take care of them and we should not hate them and laugh at them. God created them. If you love them they will help you, but if you keep on laughing you will also have a child like them.

Chocolate
Neema

My friend is called Neema. She is chocolate in colour. Clementina is also my friend from Italy. I have learned many things from her skin. If she is not taking any sun cream, she will be sick because she will have a skin infection.

Stay strong
Gladys

Change the world to be a better place for you and the people you love and care for.

In this world your words are your command. Your imagination can change the world. You just have to focus on it.

It doesn't matter what people will think of you or say about you. I know people are different with different ideas. Don't change someones ideas to be yours because that isn't meant for you. Always have a positive thought towards yourself. The world belongs to everyone, not just one person. Ignore what they say about you, they aren't you. You have to be yourself for the best of everthing. You aren't perfect, neither am I. You have to expose what you have but don't try anything you can't.

Always be yourself, it doesn't matter what comes your way. You have to fight for what you want but remember: success does not come on a silver plate. You have to struggle. Your skin doesn't matter, always seek for wisdom which helps you to stay away from discrimmination, find ways of controlling your temper, don't hunger overcome you. It may lead you to sin. Be careful with people you walk around with or having fun with. They can turn their back on you without you realising. Be like a lamp which always lights the dark. What I am trying to say is: be the light for the hopeless, be the burning flame to the helpless. It will light more and more with its blazing.

My question
Zulfa

Hi, my name is Zulfa. I want to talk about skin colour. It is very sad that some people are Albinos. Why are some people brown, black, and some are Albinos? Why? This is my questions. This is bad, this is not right. Look at the differences.

Colours
Wilbrodah

We are all the same in this world. All the colours of our skins doesn't matter – whether black or white. We should love each other. We are all created as the same person. No one in this world is more special than the other. We are all equal. We all have the same colour of the blood.

Words from an auntie
Evelyn

My name is Evelyn and I work at Child of Mercy Childrens Home. I really love my job while staying with the kids and let them feel that they are being loved. The children really need a lot of support from you guys. May the almighty God be with you all. Bye.

Table of contents